Read to Me...

Our True Beginning

Ruby Shaffer (the author) was the 1st grade teacher of MAGGIE STOLLEY's granddaughter Kathleen Littlefield in Atlanta. A gift from the Stolley-Littlefield family!

Karen Stolley

Read to Me...Our True Beginning

Written by Ruby V. Shaffer

Printed in the United States of America
Library of Congress Catalog Number: 2018963602
ISBN: 978-0-578-41202-3

Dedicated to

This book is dedicated to all of my ancestors who paved the way in order for me to be able to share with parents this vital information. I hope that the message in this book will help parents understand the magnitude and power behind reading aloud to their children. This crucial practice not only helps children to read better, but also improves their comprehension skills.

I am also dedicating this book to parents because your children did come from greatest, and that would be you. I'm sure you know that your children's potential is limitless. By helping your child develop a love for reading, you will expose them to a world of endless possibilities. Therefore, your children's outlook and purpose in life...awaits the opening of a book.

Thanks to everyone who shared a part of this journey.

Read to Me...
Our True Beginning

Written by Ruby V. Shaffer

Our beautiful beginning got lost in the mix.

Now it's time for you to know, so here's part of the fix.

Oh yes! Royalty was our name,

They called us Kings and Queens.

We must know our true past...do you know what I mean?

So take some time, take a minute, and listen to our story.

For our true history begins, with plenty of glory.

Just because things changed,

And we went through the grinder...

Does not negate our greatness, so here's the reminder.

The reminder being

We must continue to do our part.

For our children need us more than ever...

So please, let's start.

Dear Mom and Dad, sisters and brothers,
Aunties and Uncles, and all others.
Sit back and relax and listen to our rap
Because we have a story to tell.

It's up to you to make a difference
In how we lead our lives.
Our past was rough, for our history tells
All about our strife.

Over two hundred years ago we were snatched...
Snatched from our motherland.
And brought aboard crowded ships, to the U. S. A.
We had language barriers and culture shock,
But here we are today.

We were made to be slaves in this foreign land...
Were we doomed?
Like being put back in old, dry cocoons.

Sad place to be, after being free...
Free Beautiful Black Butterflies.
And that my friends, is no lie.

We worked day and night, in the fields,
Picking cotton, cleaning houses,
And cooking master's meals.

We wanted to learn how to read,
But that was against the rules.
We were beaten badly or even to death
If caught in our makeshift schools.

"I want to go to school: I want to learn to read."
"Pick that cotton and pick up speed."

So, we worked the fields like master said
Hoping one day to be free.
Yes, it was devastating what happened to us,
But that's just a part of our history.

We finally became free in the late 1860s
With no place to be.
We had no money, because the work we did for master
Was for free.

Still struggling trying to find our way,
Now that we were free.
But freedom just did not come
With opportunity.

Many years later, laws were passed
To keep us from our rights.
We were lynched and tortured
If we tried to fight for what was right.

We couldn't vote, although we were free.
That doesn't make much sense to me!

Yes, life was still very unequal
For the former slaves.
But they lived on hope, until this day
And helped pave our way.

One crisp fall day in 1955, Rosa Parks,

Tired from constantly giving in.

She didn't want to give up her seat...

Thus, she refused to move, no she didn't bend.

This made folk mad because of this act.

So they put Rosa Parks in jail, and that's a fact.

Her action sparked some changes in our lives,

To help ease some of our hurt and strife.

The dream is still alive and what will you do,

To continue to make life better for me and you?

We told our history in a form of a rap.

Because this is how our generation adapts.

Now that you know what happened in our past...

It's your time, to make it last.

Change that is for the better,

To keep our true beginning stronger than ever.

Now that we have the chance and we're really free,

Set your priorities, and take the time and read to me...

Read to me...yes, open up your mind and read to me.

Yes, it's more to it than reading, a lot more too.

But this is the beginning of what you must do.

If you believe in me, then give me a chance.

The chance that great-great grandma and grandpa never had.

Don't let the world and strangers feed me their crumbs.

Knowledge is power and power is strength...

Help me to go the entire length.

When you feed me food, you nourish by body.

When you feed me books, you nourish my mind.

So, Mom and Dad please take the time and...

Read to me, read to me...

Yes, open up my mind and read to me.

The critical years for me to learn
Are from birth through seven.
So Mom and Dad don't wait around
Until I'm eleven.

I may be a doctor or maybe a cop.
Won't know my full potential if you don't stop.
Stop and take some of your time and...
Read to me...it helps me learn you see.

Read to me daily if you can,

Or five times a week will expand

My knowledge, comprehension,

My desire to learn so I can earn my own way...

So please start today.

Remember make it fun, not just a drill.

Even though we know it's a skill.

Talk about the story while you read aloud to me.

It helps me understand and comprehend you see.

Read to me...read to me...open up my mind and read to me.

Nearly a million kids drop out of school every year,

Simply because they can't read.

So Mom and Dad help me to succeed,

By reading to me, it helps me learn you see.

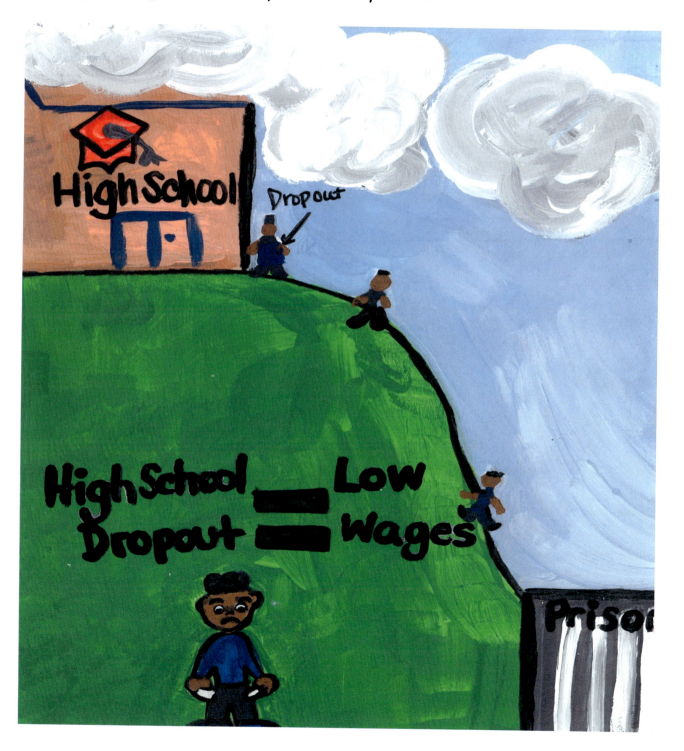

So, fill our heads with knowledge, morals,

And critical thinking skills

While we're still young.

This will last longer than any name brand.

Then I can really jump higher than my favorite sport's man.

Higher with knowledge that you take me,

By simply taking the time and read to me...

Yes, open up my mind and read to me.

This knowledge will last longer than anything you buy.

Then I do not have to reach for a handout...

But reach for the sky.

Now keep listening for we're on a roll,

And we must get our story told.

You can start reading to me while I'm still in your womb.

Yes, reading to me can never happen too soon.

Now you just gave birth to a baby boy and girl.

They're the prettiest little babies in the whole wide world.

Now your work has only just begun,

And believe it or not, it's not all fun.

You're about to take on the most challenging job

In this here world...

Raising your beautiful babies, your boy and girl.

You change their diapers, you walk the floor,

You mend their booboos,

But they still need more.

Read to me...read to me...

Open up my mind and read to me.

My vessel's empty just waiting for some knowledge.

Who and what's going to fill it?

I want to go to college.

Will it be the video games, cell phones, or even my peers?

My dear parents, do you hear?

True learning begins at home,

Where it belongs.

HELP YOUR CHILD DEVELOP A LOVE FOR READING

So help me get a jump start in this here world.

By exposing me to knowledge,

Your little baby boy and girl.

I know I'm cute and that's a fact.

But remember Mom and Dad I need more than that.

Read to me, read to me...open up my mind and read to me.

Read to me, read to me...challenge my thinking and read to me.

The public library is the place to be...
Won't cost you a dime
Because it's all free.

SCIENCE FICTION...

BIOGRAPHIES...

NON-FICTION...

FAIRY-TALES...

And there's more you see,
All you have to do is read to me...
Yes, open up my mind and read to me.

"Get the picture on the role you play?
Almost you say!"

By reading to me my vocabulary increased.
Now my teachers say I'm smart.
They said I've learned to listen and I now comprehend,
But I didn't from the start.

You've made learning fun and interesting,
Because you finally took the time and you
Read to me, yes you read to me.

Now school is not so bad and I can keep still.

The lesson we just learned was about the wheel.

You know the books you read to me the other day,

Made the lesson quite easy, I must say.

I had prior knowledge about the wheel.

I even helped the class learn a new skill.

I was proud of myself and let out a smile.

Thanks Mom and Dad for going the extra mile.

All of this happened, believe it or not...

Simply because you did stop.

And you read to me, it helped me learn you see!

So next December under the tree...

Buy me some books so you can read to me.

Yes, open up your mind and read to me.

Our ancestors set the standards high.
They paved the way for me to reach the sky.
So follow through and make it all come true,
By reading to me it helps me learn you see.

I know I'm cute and that's a fact,

But remember Mom and Dad it's about more than that.

Read to me, read to me, open up my mind and read to me.

Read to me, read to me, challenge my thinking and...

Read to me.

The End...

No...A new beginning

Made in the USA
Columbia, SC
23 November 2018